Not by Bread Alone

Daily Reflections for Lent 2020

Michelle Francl-Donnay

D1411842

✞
LITURGICAL PRESS
Collegeville, Minnesota

www.litpress.org

Nihil Obstat: Reverend Robert Harren, J.C.L., *Censor deputatus*

Imprimatur: ✛ Most Reverend Donald J. Kettler, J.C.L., Bishop of Saint Cloud, May 2, 2019.

Cover design by Monica Bokinskie. Cover art courtesy of Getty Images.

ISSN: 1552-8782

ISBN: 978-0-8146-6365-3   978-0-8146-6390-5 (ebook)

Introduction

I began writing these reflections on the summer solstice, on the day my hemisphere of the earth is flooded with as much light as it can bear. Every day that passes after the solstice, I'm more aware of the light slipping away, of the days growing inexorably dimmer, and my longing for the light to return grows stronger.

Lent enkindles similar feelings in me. My soul feels dimmed, diminished. I long for the Light that set me aflame at my baptism, yearn to be purified again in its crucible and gentled in its warmth. So Lent sends me searching for light in the Scriptures, in my prayer, and in my sisters and brothers. For light is how God broke into the world in the first place. Let there be light, he said. He offered the life of his Son to be the Light of the human race. A light to shine in the darkness, a light the darkness cannot overcome. Light is what heralded the resurrection, an angel whose arrival shook the earth, shining as bright as lightning in the dimness of a garden at dawn.

I pray in Lent for God's light to break into my life, to light the path forward. But Lent's light is more than what we receive. It's about who we are, and what we should be about. In his poem "Sowing Light," Alden Solovy turns a line from Psalm 97—*Light is sown for the just* (v. 11)—back on itself. Light is what the just must sow, in healing, in blessing, in love, prays Solovy. This is the light we are given. This is the light we must sow. This light, we will hear in the Easter *Exsultet*, will never be dimmed in the sharing.

This Lent, let us long for light: for the light sown in us, for the light sown by us, for the Light sown for us, for a light that will set us aflame. Let us long to be light itself.

Reflections

Abandoned to Grace

Readings: Joel 2:12-18; 2 Cor 5:20–6:2; Matt 6:1-6, 16-18

Scripture:
[W]e might become the righteousness of God in him. (2 Cor 5:21b)

Reflection: The Latin version of the opening prayer for Mass today uses the word *inchoare*, from which we get the English "inchoate," suggesting the barest hint of a beginning, a sketch of what might be built on this foundation, a plan for the days to follow.

The start of my Lent always feels full of plans, spiritual and otherwise. I have plans for penance and time with God; there are liturgical plans and rehearsals; plans for how my students and I will reach the end of the semester. Most of these plans will come to fruition more or less as I laid them out. My sixty-odd general chemistry students will learn to calculate the pH of an acidic solution. I will go to confession more often and give up tucking a bit of chocolate into my lunch for forty days. There will be a chaotic rehearsal for Holy Thursday and a moving celebration of the Easter Vigil. No mystery here, just my regular forty-day foray into spiritual renewal.

But I wonder if with all these plans, however reasonable they might be, I'm entirely missing the point of what Lent celebrates: the mystery that is Christ's walk to Jerusalem, into his passion, death, and resurrection, into an unimaginable reality. In a letter to Ascanio Colonna, St. Ignatius of Loyola noted, "There are very few people who realize what God would make of them if they abandoned themselves into his hands, and let themselves be formed by his grace." Can I cease making of Lent an organized campaign to banish sin from my life and instead abandon myself entirely to God's mysterious working? Can I simply fall into Lent, unsure of how I will emerge, other than with arms outstretched?

Meditation: How can you leave space for God to work in your life this Lent? What aspects of your life are you willing to abandon entirely to God's grace? Take a few moments to pray for the grace to let go of your desires for this time and enter into what God desires for you.

Prayer: Grant us the courage, O Lord, to abandon ourselves entirely into your hands for these Lenten days. Give us the joy of your Holy Spirit, and sustain us with your Word.

Facing the Cross

Readings: Deut 30:15-20; Luke 9:22-25

Scripture:
"If anyone wishes to come after me, he must deny himself and take up his cross daily and follow me." (Luke 9:23b)

Reflection: I regularly take up a cross. As an altar server I often carry the cross in procession. I stand at the end of the main aisle, holding a cross that is taller than I am by half and weighty enough to feel it in my shoulders as I raise it high so that it can be seen above the heads of the assembly. And as I lead the procession down the aisle, I cannot help but think about the less literal crosses that I will have to lift in my life. Will they make my shoulders ache? Will I be able to balance them as I walk? Where must I take them?

My eyes inevitably go to the enormous painting of Christ crucified that hangs above the century-old marble altar in my parish church. Each time I hold the cross aloft, I am brought face-to-face with Christ's suffering, face-to-face with Christ in the tabernacle, face-to-face with Christ in the people of God assembled there. I walk without a hymnal, so the only words I have to take along for this journey are what are already in my heart and head. I will surely falter on the second verse. Clothed in white, a reminder of my baptismal garment, hands and face raised up, I walk. I walk toward boundless mercy. Will this be what my last walk will be like, from this life into the next, stripped of words and pretenses, face-to-face with God and surrounded by those who have gone before me—praying not to falter? Take up your cross, says Christ, and follow me, for this is the road to eternal life, and I will not let you fall.

Meditation: To carry a cross is not just to bear the weight but to have a destination. Where are the crosses you carry taking you? What are you walking toward?

Prayer: Grant us, O Lord, the grace to take up the crosses that present themselves to us this day. And at the end, may we once more lift up the cross and in the company of the saints and angels follow you into eternal life.

Light Breaks Forth

Readings: Isa 58:1-9a; Matt 9:14-15

Scripture:
Then your light shall break forth like the dawn,
  and your wound shall be quickly healed. (Isa 58:8)

Reflection: I have a bowl of water-worn rocks on my desk, picked out of streams and off beaches as far away as Japan and as close to home as New Jersey. When the afternoon light coming through the attic window is just right, some of them seem to glow with an inner light of their own. As a scientist, I can explain the phenomenon: the light is being reflected, not like a mirror from the surface, but softly scattered in all directions by millions of microscopic cracks within the rock. This light seems to linger around the rocks. I want to cradle them in my hands and let their warmth soak in, easing the aches in body and soul.

In his song "Anthem," poet and songwriter Leonard Cohen wrote that the cracks in everything are how the light gets in. Like my rocks, which would not luminesce without the myriad crevices between the crystals allowing the light to move within them, the cracks within our hearts are how the Light gets in.

Isaiah encourages us not to seal up our fractured hearts or to polish the outsides to a high gloss, but rather to make more cracks, to break open our hearts, so that the Light can get in—and out again. The light isn't meant to merely illuminate what is around us, but to be a light that surrounds us, easing the aches of sin's burdens, sustaining us. The light that Isaiah imagines breaking forth from our crushed hearts is the light by which we see each other, that we might untie the thongs of those unjustly bound, clothe the naked, and feed the hungry.

Meditation: What faults are you tempted to wish polished away? How might they instead become spaces for the light of Christ to enter in and be reflected to those in need?

Prayer: Accept as a sacrifice, O Lord, our broken hearts and our crushed spirits. May your light spill forth from within us, that we might warm the hearts of those in despair and tend the wounds of the world.

To Ride on the Heights

Readings: Isa 58:9b-14; Luke 5:27-32

Scripture:
Then you shall delight in the LORD,
    and I will make you ride on the heights of the earth.
    (Isa 58:14b)

Reflection: On a very hot and sticky summer day, I took an afternoon walk along a section of the Appian Way where the two-thousand-year-old road descends to the crater floor of a dormant volcano, laced with vineyards and olive groves. At the crossroads I decided to take the path up to Arricia, perched on the edge of the old crater. The path is steep, climbing sixteen stories in less than a quarter of a mile. I was hot, thirsty, and uncertain if I had taken the correct fork early on. I was nearly ready to give up any chance of a view and walk back the way I had come when I turned a last corner and popped out into a seventeenth-century street behind Sancta Maria dell'Assunta. In front of me was a very modern sign: "Ascensore, 1 euro." Elevator, 1 euro. I needn't have walked at all.

There would have been no choice when Isaiah was writing. The only way to reach the heights of the earth, to catch a glimpse of the breathtaking enormity of the world around one, was to walk up to them, on trails that were hot and dusty, or cold and steep and windblown, huffing and puffing. It can be hard to imagine in these days of trams and express elevators how inaccessible the high places could be. We are being promised something unimaginable to Isaiah: that we could ascend to such heights with ease.

Today we are facing Lent's heights, walking paths that demand much of us and promise more. But we walk knowing that it is not solely our efforts that will bring us at last to the mountaintop where we can delight in the Lord, but that we can and must turn to God and ask for a lift. Jesus has come, not for the self-righteous but for those who need his help.

Meditation: What heights do you seek during this Lenten season? What perspective do you need to find in your life? Where are you tempted to try to walk the trails alone and without help? Can you ask the Lord to carry you up to the heights so that you can see the view?

Prayer: Lord, renew our hearts this Lent. Give us the courage to ask for your help to walk once again in your path, for we can do nothing without your care.

Who Are You?

Readings: Gen 2:7-9; 3:1-7; Rom 5:12-19 or 5:12, 17-19; Matt 4:1-11

Scripture:
Then the devil took him up to a very high mountain, and showed him all the kingdoms of the world in their magnificence. (Matt 4:8)

Reflection: I'm a regular user of the social media platform Twitter. It's a great way for me to keep up, not on celebrity gossip but on the work chemists all over the world are doing. So why was Twitter serving me a tweet about a magazine profile of a nineteen-year-old about to be a billionaire? The headline read, "What Are You Doing with Your Life?"

I freely admit I didn't read the article, so I have no idea what the young woman is doing with her life, but I did read some of the twelve thousand comments on the tweet. Many people took the question literally and told the twitterverse what they were doing with their lives. The responses were priceless:

"I worked in early education."

"I'm researching new drugs for cancer."

"I raised my son as a single mother."

"I'm a mother and a trauma surgeon."

"I'm a priest."

The first reading from Genesis made me think again about the litany of lives and work that followed that tweet. As Lent begins, I wonder how I might answer this question five weeks from now. What will Lent have me become? What will I do differently with my life? Perhaps the answers begin with who God created me to be when he breathed life into me. St. Catherine of Siena once wrote to a young friend, discerning his life's course, that if he was who he was created to be, he could set the whole world on fire. I hear in today's psalm (51) the desires God has for me. For a steadfast heart. For joy. For love. And the fruits of these? Eternal life.

Meditation: The *Catechism of the Catholic Church* (358) tells us we are created to love and serve God and offer back to him the whole of creation. How are you loving and serving God? How are you working within the created world to return it to God? What will you do differently with your life this Lent?

Prayer: Renew within us, Lord, a steadfast spirit. Return to us the joy we had at our baptism, and grant us the courage to once again live as you desire.

Love without Limit

Readings: Lev 19:1-2, 11-18; Matt 25:31-46

Scripture:
"When did we see you a stranger and welcome you,
or naked and clothe you?" (Matt 25:38)

Reflection: My youngest son was walking across his college campus when he encountered a group handing out leaflets. "Are you saved?" they demanded. When he declined a pamphlet, they told him, "You are going to hell." He called me that evening to tell me the story. "You're the theologian," he said, "what should I have said?"

"Matthew 25," I told him. Today's gospel. Who will be saved? Those who feed the hungry and offer water to the thirsty. Who do not brush past the beggar or fail to care for the sick. I note that Christ puts no other limits on salvation here; there is no test of dogma, no demand for particular kinds of worship. Care for the stranger. I note, too, that Christ puts no limits on who we should be serving. We are not asked to visit those imprisoned unjustly, but anyone imprisoned; to feed only those who are hungry through no fault of their own, but anyone who hungers; to welcome just those who have their papers in order, but any stranger in our land.

We are asked to love without limits, so that we might grasp that God's love for us is limitless. This is what saves us. Not professing a creed or even going to Mass on Sunday. In his essay "The Weight of Glory," C. S. Lewis reminds us that next to the Eucharist itself, our neighbor is the holiest thing we encounter; there are no ordinary people, every person is ablaze with God. So where do we encounter God's saving power? At every turn. How shall we be saved? By love and in loving.

Meditation: Where do you find difficulty in loving without limits? Is it with colleagues and friends, or is it harder with those whose lives you don't know? Commit to stepping outside your limits once today and doing an undeserved loving act for someone.

Prayer: Your command, O Lord, is clear, your ordinances just. Open my heart that I might love as you love, without limits.

March 3: Tuesday of the First Week of Lent

Shattered Bonds

Readings: Isa 55:10-11; Matt 6:7-15

Scripture:
Just as from the heavens
  the rain and snow come down
And do not return there
  till they have watered the earth,
  making it fertile and fruitful
. . . So shall my word be. (Isa 55:10a, 11a)

Reflection: I love looking out at my backyard when it is covered by a blanket of snow, in part because, unlike my driveway, I won't have to shovel it. But there is also a sense of expectancy, as I see in my mind's eye the daffodils and snowdrops tucked into their winter beds, waiting for spring. The snow melts gradually, softening the ground that shelters the bulbs, so that their shoots can more easily push through to the warmth of the lengthening days. But the snow does more than break up the soil and water the plants; it also feeds those tender shoots. Nitrogen in the air gets swept into the snow. Inert in this form, once nitrogen's bonds are shattered by bacteria it can fertilize the ground beneath the snowy cover.

Isaiah reminds us that God's words are more than a simple exchange between the Creator and his creation, more even than something to quench our thirst for the divine. God sends down his Word with the expectation that a garden will spring up. These words soften our hearts, releasing them from the rocky soil that prevents them from sprouting to life. They feed us, enabling us to do the work God expects of us, work that will bring the kingdom closer to hand. And like the nitrogen carried by the snow, we cannot do this work if we do not allow ourselves to be broken apart, our hearts shattered, what blocks our ears destroyed. We must pray that what falls from heaven upon us will return to God, bearing the fruit that our broken hearts fed.

Meditation: Where in your life has God's Word softened your heart? Where has it fed you? Where has it provoked you to undertake something new? What were the fruits of this labor? What in your heart do you sense God's Word pushing open today?

Prayer: Break open our hearts, O God, that we might bear good fruit. Grant that what we return to you has achieved what you have willed for us.

Sitting among Ashes

Readings: Jonah 3:1-10; Luke 11:29-32

Scripture:
. . . [T]hey proclaimed a fast and all of them, great and small, put on sackcloth. (Jonah 3:5b)

Reflection: The king of Nineveh rose from his throne, we are told, and sat in the ashes. After a fire destroyed my kitchen I, too, sat in ashes and soot. I quickly discovered it gets everywhere and does not wash away easily. I left smudges on everything I touched after the fire, on walls and clothes and my face. My grandmother's teapot was one of the few things in the kitchen that survived the conflagration unbroken, but thirty years later, one side is still stained with ashes that I could not entirely clean away.

I sometimes say I will put on "sackcloth and ashes" as a way of taking responsibility for a mistake, but I wonder if even now I understand what it might mean to deliberately wear my sins on my body in this way, visible for all to see and nearly impossible to scrub off. Do I realize that most people would give me a wide berth, not wanting the soot—or my sin—to rub off on them?

I still find it difficult to grasp how willing God is to draw close to us when we are broken and crushed in spirit. Perhaps it takes sitting in ashes, literal or metaphorical, to catch a glimpse of the immensity of the mercy the psalmist is begging for in Psalm 51, to be cleansed of sin that clings like soot and threatens to spread to everything we touch. To have made whole again what we ourselves cannot repair. God is not seeking the perfect and the polished but desires to perfect those whose hearts are contrite and spirits humble. God will not hesitate to reach out for us, ashes or sins notwithstanding.

Meditation: Like soot, sin leaves its fingerprints on our lives, even when the original breach is over and done with. Where do you most need God's help in cleaning up the residue of a transgression?

Prayer: All-merciful God, your people long for hands and hearts clean of sin. Accept our contrite hearts and humbled spirits, and bring us to perfection.

Carved Anew

Readings: Esth C:12, 14-16, 23-25; Matt 7:7-12

Scripture:
When I called, you answered me;
    you built up strength within me. (Ps 138:3)

Reflection: Give me courage, prayed Esther in her anguish. Build up strength within me, cries the psalmist. The night my first husband died, I sought refuge in the psalms. Not knowing what else to pray for in those dark hours, I prayed for courage, I prayed for strength, I prayed that God would not forsake me or Tom.

Weeks later, shattered by grief, weighted down by the details of death, car titles, and probate court, I returned again and again to this image of God building up strength within me, of God somehow repairing the damage done. I recalled the story of Michelangelo's carving of David. The block of marble Michelangelo used had a huge gash in it from a previous sculptor's attempt to carve it; it was unclear if anything could be made from it.

Michelangelo, however, could see the possibilities within this block of marble, risky as they were. He carved David at an angle within the block, using the gouge to set David's stance, rather than trying to fill it in, and unsure if it could stand on its own at the last. So, too, I realized that God could see the possibilities in me. He would not repair the great gash Tom's death had made in my life but instead worked with it, carving carefully at odd angles until he risked setting me on my feet again. I would not be the same as I was before, but if I could bear with the Sculptor, I would at the last stand.

This Lent I pray for such courage as Esther had, for the willingness to be set askew, to let God refashion my life around the wounds that sin has left. To bear with the Sculptor while he makes of me a new creation.

Meditation: Though we long to erase sin and its effect from our lives, we cannot always undo its effects. Where has God worked around sin's gouges in your life to re-create you? Where do you most need God to reshape your life this Lent?

Prayer: Build up your strength within us, O God. Do not forsake the work of your hands, but refashion our lives that we might once again stand upright in your presence.

Reaching Out of the Depths

Readings: Ezek 18:21-28; Matt 5:20-26

Scripture:
Out of the depths I cry to you, O LORD;
LORD, hear my voice! (Ps 130:1-2a)

Reflection: I once spent a week in a hermitage on the edge of a cliff in California. The view out to sea and down to the bay 1,700 feet below was amazing. But each morning the bay filled with fog. I would stand in the tiny garden and look down into a seemingly bottomless, roiling abyss, and the first lines of Psalm 130 would run through my mind, "Out of the depths I cry to you, O LORD, / . . . hear my voice!"

Every morning I walked down the road, deeper into the clammy darkness. Yet when I would walk back up the road, the light from above would be coming through, diffusing through the mist until the very air glowed. It was a potent reminder to turn back when I find myself in the depths and reach out for God. To learn how to orient myself within the heaving depths, where I cannot see the way forward nor be sure I have found solid ground on which to stand. Turn toward me, God says, and I will reach into the depths of your sin and pull you out. Trust me, for surely as dawn comes every day, I will redeem you.

God is on more than a rescue mission here, also modeling for us in the gospel how we should act with each other. We are to listen for each other's cries for mercy and for justice. We should not be afraid to reach out to those we have wronged and to those we have been wronged by, and trust that there is mercy in abundance, enough for us all. We must strive to pull each other out of the depths.

Meditation: Where do you hear cries for mercy emerging from the depths? In your own life or in the lives of others? Who can you reach out to today to forgive or to seek forgiveness from?

Prayer: The dawn can seem far away, O Lord, and we struggle to see your light on the horizon. Draw us up from the depths and from the darkness into your mercy. Give us the strength to reach out for our sisters and brothers in need.

Today

Readings: Deut 26:16-19; Matt 5:43-48

Scripture:
Today you are making this agreement with the LORD: he is to be your God and you are to walk in his ways. (Deut 26:17a)

Reflection: After a series of writing projects, my study at home was a mess. For weeks I had been saying I'd clean it up on the weekend. But the weekend would arrive and something seemingly more urgent would come up, and the piles on desk, floor, and shelves would grow ever more unruly. The time never seemed right and the task frankly impossible. Besides, I'd grown comfortable with the clutter.

I hear in the readings today a call to move, to get out of my comfort zone. Not at some vague future moment, but now, today. This day, God says, you are my people. This day, says Moses, you will walk in God's way. Today you will love those who hate you, pray for those who persecute you.

I want to say, "Wait, not yet, I'm not prepared to take on such an enormous project." It's early days in Lent, so there is time. The first reading pushes me to recognize that now is the acceptable time, that today is the day I must commit to walking in the Lord's pathway. Today is the moment to step away from the sins that I have become too comfortable with. And while it's tempting to think that walking in the way of perfection is an impossible task, one that even if I began I could never manage, I find consolation in the readings. This call, says Jesus, is not to instant perfection but to get moving, to walk with purpose in the direction of God. To take not just one step but a second and a third.

Meditation: What seems insurmountably difficult to undertake this Lent? Are there well-worn habits you wish to change or long-standing conflicts you wish at last to resolve? Ask God what one small, manageable step you can take today to move in that direction. What are the next small steps?

Prayer: God, you have given us the law and the prophets that we might know how to walk in your ways. Do not forsake us, but help us on the way to perfection.

March 8: Second Sunday of Lent

A Tender Attentiveness

Readings: Gen 12:1-4a; 2 Tim 1:8b-10; Matt 17:1-9

Scripture:
But Jesus came and touched them, saying, "Rise, and do not be afraid." (Matt 17:7)

Reflection: When I listen to these familiar stories of our salvation, of the founding of Israel with Abram, of the transfiguration, I sometimes want to do as Peter, James, and John did and throw myself facedown on the ground and cover my eyes. I'm awestruck not so much by the immensity of the promises made to a childless seventy-five-year-old man or by the voice coming from the cloud—as overwhelming as these may be—but by God's tenderness in these encounters.

God's strength and power cannot help but shake us to our foundation. Yet in both these encounters he seeks not to intimidate, instead proffering kindness and compassion in the midst of overpowering experiences. God blesses Abram again and again, so much so, he assures Abram, that these blessings will spill over to every community on earth. Jesus comes over to the apostles sprawled and trembling on the ground and touches them, reassuring them. We place our trust not in a God who terrifies us but in a God whose kindness and mercy are ever present.

In her *Showings*, St. Julian of Norwich calls God our clothing, who wraps and enfolds us in a tender love. God, she says, never promised that we wouldn't be tempest-tossed and frightened. He did promise he will never let us go.

We, too, are called to a tender attentiveness to each other in challenging times. We are called to realize that we are blessed no less than Abram was, so that God's blessings might continue to overflow, that we might be blessings to all the world. We are called to do as Christ did on the mountaintop and reach out to our sisters and brothers living in fear and trembling—to never let them go.

Meditation: When has God reached out to you with a tender attentiveness? How do you see the ways in which God has blessed you spilling over and reaching out to the larger community you live in?

Prayer: Lord, be tender with us, enfolding us in your love. Help us to be tender with each other, reaching out to those who live in fear and carrying your blessings to the ends of the earth.

Mercy-ing

Readings: Dan 9:4b-10; Luke 6:36-38

Scripture:
"Be merciful, just as your Father is merciful." (Luke 6:36)

Reflection: Pope Francis's motto is *Miserando atque eligendo*. Its English translations, such as "by having mercy," sound awkward and unfinished to my ears. It doesn't translate any better into Spanish, Pope Francis's mother tongue, so to capture the sense he desired, the pope coined a new word in Spanish—*misericordiando*. "Mercy-ing" in English. Mercy, suggests the pope, is not an object to be given but an action to be undertaken. Think of it as a verb, not a noun.

Mercy was once a verb in English. It meant to be grateful, not in general but for particular gifts; it meant to stir up the desire to be merciful to others. I wonder if Pope Francis is trying to recapture for us this sense of gratitude and mercy that spills over. He reminds us that God's mercy is not meted out in dribs and drabs to the deserving. Nor ought it be hoarded for the most desperate cases, but mercy is an unending font of forgiveness and grace for all those who thirst for it.

I'm reminded of one of the stories told about the Desert Father Abba Bessarion, a sixth-century saint and ascetic. He was walking along the seashore with one of his students, who complained of being thirsty. "Drink some of the sea water," Bessarion told him. To the student's surprise, the water he scooped up was fresh. He drank his fill then immediately began filling his canteen in case he became thirsty later. "Why?" wondered Bessarion. "There is no need. God is here, God is everywhere."

Be merciful, says the gospel. Be grateful for the gift of mercy received, and so be merciful in return: be mercy-ing. For mercy is ours to drink, everywhere and at all times.

Meditation: Where do you thirst for mercy? Do you trust God to be merciful? Are there times when you have worried that God's mercy is limited? How have you shared God's boundless mercy with others?

Prayer: God of mercy and compassion, we thirst for forgiveness. Let your mercy be upon us, that we might be signs of your saving power to all the world.

Seized by God

Readings: Isa 1:10, 16-20; Matt 23:1-12

Scripture:
Come now, let us set things right,
    says the Lord. (Isa 1:18a)

Reflection: Why, wonders God in today's psalm (50), do we
reject discipline yet say we know and wish to keep God's
law? Discipline calls to our minds harsh punishments meted
out by rigid authorities, so it is understandably something
we shy away from, but in its original Latin sense to discipline
simply meant to teach. Though the origins of the Latin word
are lost to history, scholars speculate it comes from *capere*, to
seize, to grasp an idea or a method.

My students can be resistant to some of my idiosyncratic
approaches to teaching. In particular, they turn their noses
up at my instructions to draw figures by hand. Why, they
cry, when the computer can do it in the twinkle of an eye
and much more precisely? But I want them to grapple with
the equation, not just with their mind's eye but to grab it
with their hands, to feel its peaks and valleys, to know the
space it occupies. I'm less interested in a perfect representa-
tion than I am in relationships: Do they grasp how this equation expresses what we can observe in the real world?

Jesus is asking the disciples to be disciplined in their lives, to do more than recite the rules but to work to humbly live them out in the messiness of the world. He wants them to understand viscerally the ups and downs of living the Christian life, to take it into their hands, to seize it. He echoes Isaiah: this is an invitation to work with God, to set things right not on our own but in God's company. To let God seize them, capture their hearts as well as their minds.

Meditation: Where do you lean on following "the rules" rather than reach for a deeper understanding of how Christ is suggesting you should live? In what situations do you find it most difficult to see what God desires? Can you ask God to help you set things right in your heart as well as your mind?

Prayer: Seize our hearts and our minds, O Lord, and help us to set things aright. Extend your hand to us, and show us your saving power.

God Always and in Everything

Readings: Jer 18:18-20; Matt 20:17-28

Scripture:
[W]hoever wishes to be first among you shall be your slave.
(Matt 20:26)

Reflection: A neighbor stopped me in the grocery store, saying, "Congratulations!" When I looked puzzled, she elaborated, "I heard you were named chair of the department, what an honor." Oh, it's not what you think, I said. It's less being in charge and more being of service: I go to meetings and write memos so that my colleagues don't need to.

I hear Jesus in Matthew's gospel asking James and John—the sons of Zebedee—where they wish to stand. He's not offering seats of honor, but the chance to be servants, to give up their very lives to save the lives of others. He wants them to shift their perspective away from themselves and onto others, away from themselves and onto God.

It reminds me of what St. Vincent Pallotti, who like me was a college professor, once wrote in his diary:

Not the goods of the world, but God.
Not riches, but God.
Not honors, but God.
Not distinction, but God.
Not dignities, but God.

Not advancement, but God.
God always and in everything.

I keep St. Vincent's litany of desires on my desktop, to help me find my perspective amid the many demands of my day and to remind me what I should long for: God, always and in everything.

Meditation: What temptations of your own might you add to St. Vincent's litany? What keeps you from desiring God always and in everything?

Prayer: Help us keep our eyes fixed on you, O Lord. Let us not desire riches nor strive for honors, but seek you in all things and at all times.

March 12: Thursday of the Second Week of Lent

A Parable in Real Time

Readings: Jer 17:5-10; Luke 16:19-31

Scripture:
Lying at his door was a poor man named Lazarus, covered with sores, who would gladly have eaten his fill of the scraps that fell from the rich man's table. (Luke 16:20-21a)

Reflection: It was a bitter cold morning in Washington, D.C. A man in a green canvas coat was huddled against a fence near the corner of Capitol and E Streets, hands pushed deep into his pockets. A man in a black wool coat came striding down the street, briefcase in one hand, bagel in the other. As he reached the corner, he blithely tossed his half-eaten bagel into a nearby trash can and crossed the street without missing a step. As the bagel sailed through the air, the first man stood, took two quick steps toward the trash can, reached in, pulled out the bagel, and bit into it. The light changed and the taxi I was sitting in drove on.

Almost a decade later I can still feel how all the air was sucked out of my lungs as I watched the parable of Lazarus and the Rich Man and his uneaten scraps play out before my eyes. I can still hear the questions swirling in my head. How hungry do you have to be to pull a half-eaten piece of bread from the garbage on the street? Does the man who threw the bagel away have any idea how hungry the man he just walked past was? But the question I have kept wondering about all these years is what *I* should have done. Should I have stopped the taxi I was in, gotten out and given the man all the money I had in my bag? Handed over my warm gloves and scarf? Should I have taken him for breakfast?

I'm quite sure the answer to all the last questions is yes. And I did none of that, despite having heard this parable from one who has risen from the dead. Forgive me, I pray. Again and again.

Meditation: Where have you seen this parable playing out in your life? What do you unthinkingly discard that someone else desperately needs? How could you help see that their needs are met with dignity?

Prayer: Forgive us, O Lord, our inability to see those around us in need. Help us to care for each other with tenderness and dignity.

March 13: Friday of the Second Week of Lent

Holy Daring

Readings: Gen 37:3-4, 12-13a, 17b-28a; Matt 21:33-43, 45-46

Scripture:
The stone that the builders rejected
  has become the cornerstone. (Matt 21:42b)

Reflection: Joseph's brothers hated his dreams, hated the idea that the youngest among them might one day rule them; they hated his dreams so much they plotted to kill him. But still Joseph dared to dream. He dared to think that these were holy dreams, that the Lord might have some work for him to do.

What might happen if we dared to dream with God? What could we build that is marvelous to behold? I wonder how often I disregard God's messengers—whether they come in dreams or run into me in the aisle at the grocery store—mocking myself for thinking God would come to me in this way. Or worse yet, dismissing the messenger or message as outlandish.

The chapel next to my office has a relic of St. Thérèse of Lisieux on the tiny altar. St. Thérèse also dared to dream, to dream that she could become a Carmelite sister, boldly proclaiming in prayer that God's mercy was infinite and that every step on her "little way" mattered, that every person mattered.

Theologian Karl Rahner, SJ, wrote in a reflection, "God of My Daily Routine," that the way to God must lead through the middle of our ordinary lives. So my dreams with God are small ones, of little steps on the way, like St. Thérèse's. I dream not of great spiritual insights, but of time to drift silently with God. I dream not of changing the world, but of changing my corner of it enough that the little ones in the shelter have their own beds to sleep in. Still, to dream that God is at work in my life at all is a bold dream indeed.

Meditation: What small and utterly outlandish thing is God asking of you today? Is it letting someone with a full cart go ahead of you in line at the grocery store? Listen for his voice coming out of the darkness, and dare to take one step along the way.

Prayer: God, grant that I might hear your voice even in my dreams. Give me the courage to boldly walk in your ways, to take the steps, large and small, that bring your kingdom ever closer.

Channels of Mercy

Readings: Mic 7:14-15, 18-20; Luke 15:1-3, 11-32

Scripture:
Who is there like you, the God
. . . [w]ho does not persist in anger forever,
but delights rather in clemency? (Mic 7:18)

Reflection: As I came through the door of the retreat house kitchen, an elderly Jesuit was rummaging through a drawer, a bowl and a bag of cereal on the counter in front of him. Stymied at last in his search for scissors, he grabbed the bag and pulled. It promptly exploded, sending cereal raining down.

As I helped him clean up the mess, he told me that during his novitiate he was taught that when a common item went missing, to consider whoever had it must have had a greater need for it than you did. He admitted he said it more often with sarcasm than with mercy. I've thought of that chance advice more times than I can count over the years. Still, when faced with a missing kitchen item, I all too often start grumbling like the older brother in the parable of the Prodigal Son. After all, I did the right thing and put it away, so I deserve to be able to find it now!

Both the Jesuit and I are correct: we have done the right thing; we simply have misunderstood what our motivation should be. Are we doing what is right because we expect right in return? Or do we do what is right so those more in need might find a paring knife or scissors—or forgiveness. Acts of mercy are not an exchange of favors, a grudging transaction. They are unexpected pools in the desert, filled by what has overflowed from God's hands—and run through ours. We are created to be channels of mercy, not scorekeepers.

Meditation: Are there times when you have offered mercy grudgingly or withheld it because it had not been offered to you? Can you see yourself not as the source of mercy but as its conduit?

Prayer: You, O Lord, are the source of all mercy. Help us to be ever more open channels of your grace and forgiveness to our brothers and sisters.

We Are Living Water

Readings: Exod 17:3-7; Rom 5:1-2, 5-8; John 4:5-42 or 4:5-15, 19b-26, 39a, 40-42

Scripture:
Jesus said to her, "Give me a drink." (John 4:7b)

Reflection: I thirst. I thirst for the living God. Like the Samaritans who beg for Jesus to stay with them awhile, I long for living water, to have my thirst assuaged forever from God's inexhaustible spring. Who would not?

But this gospel opens with *Jesus* thirsting. Not only for water but for us. God is seeking believers. Jesus tells the woman that God is looking for those who "will worship him in Spirit and in truth." We may long for God, but God longed for us first. If only I could grasp this reality. Like all of us, I am flawed. Like the woman at the well, God knows the truth about me, whether I will admit it or not. And so, like the woman, I am surprised that Jesus would seek me out, would thirst for anything I might have to offer.

In reflecting on this gospel, St. Augustine suggested that the water Jesus sought was the woman's faith. When he drank of that faith, she was brought into his Body, into the church. What is Christ seeking in me? A living faith, a faith entirely subsumed into his life, a faith that overflows into my community. A faith that brings with it gifts to be used for the good of Christ's Body, for the church. I am astonished that God—the all-powerful God—thirsts for the talents we have, large and small.

Living water isn't stagnant, it flows, and what I am flows into these inexhaustible waters, to be brought to life in its currents, carried to places I cannot imagine, satisfying the thirst of Christ's Body with the gifts he has given me.

Meditation: Which of your gifts do you think the church is thirsting for? Is anything impeding your ability to allow Christ to put them at the service of his Body? Consider asking God for the grace to become living water.

Prayer: Enlighten our minds, O God, that we might know our strengths as well as our weaknesses. Help us to draw living water from Christ's inexhaustible well, that we might use our gifts to quench the thirst of our brothers and sisters.

Getting the Message

Readings: 2 Kgs 5:1-15a; Luke 4:24-30

Scripture:
Send forth your light and your fidelity;
   they shall lead me on
And bring me to your holy mountain,
   to your dwelling-place. (Ps 43:3)

Reflection: When I get dressed in my finest to go to Mass on a Sunday, I expect (and usually get) a homily that breaks open the Word proclaimed. But I'm reminded by the story of Naaman that preaching is not confined to the expected, to the people and places where we routinely seek it out. Instead, God's Word is on the loose, preaching on street corners and found in the mouths of those we don't see as prophet or priest. Yet by virtue of our baptism, we are all priest and prophet, we are all God's Word set loose in the world.

We need to look for the light, have an ear for the truth, whether spoken by a priest vested on a Sunday in a bright church, or by the guy at the halfway house who played jazz tunes for me while I single-handedly cooked a dinner for forty. "I have a message for you from the Holy Spirit," he said, and he turned up the music. Malcolm Muggeridge, a journalist and twentieth-century Christian apologist, pointed out that everything that happens to us is a parable where God speaks to us. The art of life, he said, is to get the message.

"When shall I see the face of God?" wonders the psalm for the day. Today. And tomorrow, and the next day. I suspect that this is the message God had for me on that summer day the Holy Spirit inspired an elderly DJ to play tunes for a shorthanded cook in a hot and steamy kitchen in Philadelphia: The face of God is always before you.

Meditation: Psalm 43 asks God to send forth his light and his truth, to guide us to his dwelling place. Where has that light shown you the face of God in an unexpected place today? What message did God have for you? How do you imagine others see and hear God through you?

Prayer: Send forth your light and truth, O Lord, that I might see your face in those I meet and hear your Word proclaimed on street corners and in kitchens. May you lead me to the place where you dwell, that I might sing your praises forever.

Living on Mercy

Readings: Dan 3:25, 34-43; Matt 18:21-35

Scripture:
Peter approached Jesus and asked him, "Lord, if my brother sins against me, how often must I forgive him?" (Matt 18:21a)

Reflection: "What's your policy on late homework?" wonders the student at my door. After years of teaching, I know this question is often not so much a request for a number—the percentage I take off each day work is late—as it is a precursor to a plea for mercy.

Reflecting on Matthew's story of Peter's question to Jesus, I wonder what prompted Peter to ask Jesus about forgiving, again and again. I feel certain it wasn't a rhetorical question or even a request for information. Who did he feel he'd already forgiven enough? Was it someone he'd forgiven many times, and yet again and again he found his trust betrayed? Or was it Peter who had transgressed and needed an open hand to forgive him?

I want to place myself in the story as the one forgiving, as someone who is already generous with forgiveness but asked to be more generous yet. As formidable as that can be when I want to wrap my righteous indignation around me like a cloak, it's even more difficult for me to see myself as the one in need of forgiveness from my brothers and sisters and from

God. Not once or seven times, not even seventy times seven. But as many times as it takes. It means admitting I'm a sinner. Harder still, it means admitting I live utterly on the mercy of God.

Meditation: Denise Levertov's poem "To Live in the Mercy of God" invokes the image of a waterfall, pounding for eons upon the rocks below, as an image of God's love wearing away at our resisting hearts. What rock in your heart is being worn away by God's mercy, even when you are unaware of the forces within which you dwell?

Prayer: Your mercy, O Lord, knows no bounds. Grant that I can be openhanded in forgiving my sisters and brothers. May I be humble enough to know how often and deeply I am forgiven by you.

Taking the Hint

Readings: Deut 4:1, 5-9; Matt 5:17-19

Scripture:
"Do not think that I have come to abolish the law or the prophets." (Matt 5:17a)

Reflection: I was in first grade when I baked my first cake. Naturally I chose the most complicated chocolate cake recipe in the cookbook, which included the mysterious-to-me instruction to add the water alternately with the dry ingredients. Why can't I just put all the flour in at once, I asked my mother. She didn't know but suggested it was unwise to ignore the instructions without knowing what lay behind them.

St. Augustine suggested in a fifth-century sermon on the First Letter of St. John that all of the law and Jesus' instructions to us could be summed up in one short line: "Love, and do what you will." But here, in Matthew's gospel, Jesus seems to be focusing on the minutiae rather than the big picture: observe even the smallest part of the letter of the law. We must stick to the instructions, Jesus says, even if we do not see the sense in them, until the law is truly fulfilled.

The law is not an arbitrary set of rules to trip us up, but a way to train us in God's ways, to show us what salvation looks like, to help us to act in love when we do not feel like loving. In his poem "The Dry Salvages," T. S. Eliot points out we do not have God's perspective; we have only hints. For the rest, he wrote, we have prayer and observance and discipline. These instructions are meant to guide our feet into the way of peace, until the kingdom of God is a reality. Only then will we have no need of the law or the prophets.

Meditation: What "smallest" letter of the law do you find most confining? Is it because you have outgrown the need for it or because it chafes at your failings?

Prayer: Make known to us, O Lord, your law, that you may train us in love and form us in grace. Strengthen us in our Lenten disciplines, and make us steadfast in prayer.

Unsurprised

Readings: 2 Sam 7:4-5a, 12-14a, 16; Rom 4:13, 16-18, 22; Matt 1:16, 18-21, 24a
  or Luke 2:41-51a

Scripture:
"Why were you looking for me? Did you not know that I must be in my Father's house?" (Luke 2:49b)

Reflection: Parents worry. I worry about my grown sons, even when I know I shouldn't. Joseph certainly worried about Jesus when he went missing in Jerusalem. I sometimes wonder what went through Joseph's mind when he finally came upon his son teaching in the temple. Relief, surely, both of his own nagging worries and those of Mary—they had both risked so much for this child.

The gospel says Mary and Joseph were astonished to find Jesus teaching in the temple, and I know well this sense of being stunned by what my children can do. But I wonder if they were surprised. I was astonished when my then-five-year-old plopped down next to me one morning and read aloud the first page of a new book—I had no idea he had taught himself to read. But I wasn't truly surprised, as I was expecting this next phase in his development. Surely Mary and Joseph had been waiting to see how a child they knew to be conceived through the Holy Spirit might develop. Had they been watching for signs?

Parents wait. We wait for our children to be born, we wait for them to come home. We wait to see what they will become as they grow up. God is worrying and waiting on us too. Worrying we will go missing, waiting to see what we might become, reborn as we have been in water and the Holy Spirit. And while I suspect I might in a moment of grace astonish God, God is never surprised. For I am known in the depths of my being, all my goings and all my becomings. God has seen the signs.

Meditation: What signs do you see in your life of growth that has been encouraged and sustained by the Holy Spirit during this Lent? What expectations do you have of God working in your life? What astonishes you about the work of God in the people around you?

Prayer: Tend the seeds you have planted in our hearts, O Lord, that we might grow to be what you have created us to be. Let us see the signs of what you are bringing to life, not only in ourselves but in our brothers and sisters.

The Scent of Mercy

Readings: Hos 14:2-10; Mark 12:28-34

Scripture:
His splendor shall be like the olive tree
　　and his fragrance like the Lebanon cedar. (Hos 14:7b)

Reflection: The weather is often cold and raw in March, and I long for the light and warmth of late spring, for the summer blooms that each year astound me with their abundance. The images Hosea uses to remind us of God's love and the abundance of his mercy are similarly enticing, awash with light, lush and warm. I am transported to the garden outside my mother's kitchen, where an olive tree has set deep roots, shielding the house from the unsparing desert sun. I follow the scents: my mother's roses to the rosemary that covers a hillside to the towering cedar tree planted by the back pasture. To a place to sit quietly away from the hubbub generated by siblings and nieces and nephews.

　　Hosea reminds me that signs of God's love and mercy are everywhere, leading me to a place of shelter, to the place where God dwells. God's love is rooted deeply, his mercy abundant and beautiful and fragrant. How could I not long for these places, not walk these paths, not be warmed in the light of such grace?

Today marks the halfway point in Lent. We have set our roots deep into the stories of salvation history, listened to the stories of Abraham and Moses, of Naaman and the three young men in the furnace. Soon we will take up John's gospel and follow Jesus into Jerusalem. To see him as the Son of God, coming into glory, to see him as the Redeemer, full of mercy. This is the moment for me to leave aside the world and commit to following Jesus into Jerusalem with all my heart, all my mind, and all my strength. This is the moment to stop, to breathe in Christ's fragrance and be warmed by his merciful love.

Meditation: What places do you find to be particularly redolent of God's mercy? Where do you find traces of God's glory in the world around you? What do you need to prepare yourself for in the second half of Lent?

Prayer: Open our senses to see your traces in the world around us, O Lord. Let us breathe in your strength, that we might follow you with our hearts and minds and souls into the life to come.

What Is Love?

Readings: Hos 6:1-6; Luke 18:9-14

Scripture:
For it is love that I desire, not sacrifice,
   and knowledge of God rather than burnt offerings.
      (Hos 6:6)

Reflection: "I've spent hours studying every night, how did I get such a bad grade on this exam? My roommate didn't spend half that much time," cries the student in my office. Tell me how you spend your time, I gently suggest, suspecting her honestly hard efforts are misdirected.

I hear a touch of the same dodge in the Pharisee's diatribe: "I fast! I tithe! I've put my time in." And, I'm ashamed to say, I sometimes hear it in my own words as I tell my husband, "I did the dishes. I cleaned the refrigerator. I grocery shopped." All said in a tone laced with asperity and with a subtext of "I've done this all—again—and you haven't."

It is reasonable to want our hard work and sacrifices to be recognized and rewarded. We want to get back what we put into a relationship. But love goes beyond the reasonable, beyond the contractual. *Tell me not what others did or didn't do, but tell me how you loved and how you failed to love*, I hear God gently suggesting. *Bring me a humble, contrite heart, and*

I will show you what love looks like, in all its unreasonable, immoderate abundance.

Meditation: I find Paul's famous letter to the Corinthians (1 Cor 13:4-13) on love—"Love is patient, love is kind . . ."—so often used at weddings, a provocative examination of conscience for every day. Where have I failed to be patient, where have I sought my own interests? Where, today, have I failed to love as God loves?

Prayer: God, teach us to be patient and to be kind. Teach us not to seek our own interests but to be attentive to those of our sisters and brothers. Teach us to love, immoderately and unreasonably.

Cost of Light

Readings: 1 Sam 16:1b, 6-7, 10-13a; Eph 5:8-14; John 9:1-41 or 9:1, 6-9, 13-17, 34-38

Scripture:
Live as children of light. (Eph 5:8b)

Reflection: I struggle to grasp the images in St. Paul's letter to the Ephesians. I live near a major city, where true darkness is hard to come by. Even in the middle of a dark and stormy night, there is enough light for me to read by. My astronomer colleagues bemoan the "light pollution" that blinds us to the glories of the heavens above. And light is so cheap. To brightly light a room for an hour with a modern bulb costs a few cents, but two thousand years ago, someone would have labored for hours to buy enough oil to light an entire room. Light demands little from me; I can summon it with a flick of my hand—or a word to a smart lamp.

But the light Paul is holding out to us is not like the light I know; it is not a cheap light, but the costly light of his time. Like the grace Dietrich Bonhoeffer spoke of in his essay "Costly Grace," the price of this light requires I surrender everything. The gospel tells us how Jesus opens the eyes of the man born blind, letting him see light for the first time. This light was hard to come by: his eyes smeared with mud, still blind, he had to find his way to Siloam and wash. The cost of this light was his community, who when he pro-claimed the good news of what had been done for him threw him bodily out.

What is the cost of the light that we are given to hold at our baptism, that we are asked to keep burning? This light isn't a suffused glow on the horizon, blurring the stars. This light is a flame in the darkness, held in our hands where we can feel its heat. To live with it is to be on the alert, always awake, always at risk. This is a light of great price.

Meditation: What has the light of the Gospel cost you? What would you risk to keep it alight?

Prayer: God, you have called us from darkness to be light for the world. Grant that we might burn brightly, with all that we have, a sign to the nations of your saving power.

Ask One Thing

Readings: Isa 65:17-21; John 4:43-54

Scripture:
"Unless you people see signs and wonders, you will not believe." (John 4:48b)

Reflection: When I was a young girl, I prayed each night that when I woke in the morning God would have healed my eyes so that I could see clearly. Yet each morning I awoke, still unable to read the time on the bedside clock without groping for my glasses. I eventually gave up asking for this miracle, managing to be grateful to live in a time where miraculously enough, eyeglasses had been invented.

For a long time the experience made me leery of praying for miracles, or at least for specific miracles. Perhaps I was afraid to ask for a miracle because I didn't think I was deserving of one. Perhaps I was more afraid that I didn't trust God enough, that if the miraculous ending I was seeking didn't materialize, my faith would falter. And I find it hard to reconcile the God I meet in the reading from Isaiah, who promises so much, with a God who sometimes answers the prayers of our hearts with "no" or "not yet."

In his letter to the widow Proba, St. Augustine addresses these fears. He advises not praying for each little thing, but for the one miraculous thing that is our ultimate end. In the words of the psalmist, "One thing I ask of the LORD, this I seek, / to dwell in the house of the LORD all the days of my life." Widen your horizons to desire beyond what is on earth, advises Augustine. This longing increases our capacity to receive the gifts God has for us and opens our hearts to all the miraculous possibilities around us. So perhaps the answer God wants to make to our prayers for miracles isn't "yes" or "no," but "wait, there is so much more you could want."

Meditation: Have there been times in your life when you prayed for a miracle? How did that prayer change your relationship with God? What one thing would you seek from God?

Prayer: Lord, you long to change our mourning into dancing, to wipe away our every tear. Rouse in us the desire to seek to dwell with you in joy all the days of our lives and for all eternity.

Water of Life

Readings: Ezek 47:1-9, 12; John 5:1-16

Scripture:
"Wherever the river flows, every sort of living creature that can multiply shall live." (Ezek 47:9a)

Reflection: "CHNOPS and water," said the astronomer at the Vatican Observatory Summer School. Looking for life on other planets? Look for the basic elements: **c**arbon, **h**ydrogen, **n**itrogen, **o**xygen, **p**hosphorous, and **s**ulfur, he said. And water, copious amounts of liquid water. I couldn't help but think of this passage from Ezekiel, the prophet wading ever deeper into flowing waters, a great river giving life to fish and trees, providing food and medicine for all.

The building blocks of life come in forms that can seem gritty and unappealing: chunks of rock, sticky tar, and sulfurous fumes. Yet sulfur literally gives shape to our cells, and atoms of phosphorous and oxygen pulled from minerals within the earth hold our genetic code together. Water is critical to life because it brings the other elements together, letting them move freely enough to encounter each other, react, and build something new. From these otherwise unremarkable elements come Ezekiel's fruit trees and fish, food and medicines.

We, too, are ordinary and unremarkable materials. At times it can be hard to see beneath the surface and grasp the extraordinary potential within others, and even within ourselves. Water is critical to our life as Christians. Those overflowing waters of baptism wash away the grit of original sin, freeing us to live and move within the Body of Christ, freeing us to come together as something new. There is no life without these waters, not within us, not within our community. They are what free us to feed each other and heal each other's ills.

Meditation: What have you been freed to do by virtue of your baptism? Where do you seek yet more freedom to feed the hungry or strengthen the weak? What waters are you being invited to wade into with God?

Prayer: Lead us, Lord, to see the extraordinary potential in our sisters and brothers as well as ourselves. Stir up the waters, that we might be freed to move, able to build the kingdom of God, teeming with life.

Emptied by Grace

Readings: Isa 7:10-14; 8:10; Heb 10:4-10; Luke 1:26-38

Scripture:
"Behold, I am the handmaid of the Lord.
May it be done to me according to your word." (Luke 1:38)

Reflection: *Hail Mary, full of grace.* I've been saying those words as long as I can remember. I've prayed them in desperate need at my critically ill mother's bedside, cried them in frustration as my kids fought in the backseat of the car, sung them with joy at feasts. They are tucked on holy cards in my missal. And each time they are on my tongue, I've longed to be full of grace, to be filled with the Holy Spirit as Mary was.

But to be filled with grace as Mary was means also a willingness to grasp how deeply this fullness, this grace, this very universe is rooted in emptiness. Creation itself was pulled forth from nothingness, bursting into being 13.8 billion years ago. Mary is filled with grace and the Holy Spirt, and in her ninth month, overfull with God made flesh. But in Mary's yes to this fullness, she is also saying yes to being emptied of God's Son, to let God go forth from her. It foreshadows Christ's own emptying so eloquently described by Paul in his letter to the Philippians, but it also sets a model for us.

Theologian Johann Baptist Metz argues that Christ shows us what it means to be fully human in his emptying. It follows that the core of being human is to allow ourselves to be emptied, to give ourselves not only to God but to assent to God's going forth from us. The fullness of God's work requires emptiness: Mary's, Christ's, and so ours as well.

Meditation: How do you think Mary felt after she gave birth to Jesus, after having held God within her all those months? In what ways have you held God within? In what ways have you brought God to birth?

Prayer: Hail Mary, full of grace, the Lord is with thee. Blessed art thou among women and blessed is the fruit of thy womb, Jesus. Holy Mary, Mother of God, pray for us sinners, now and at the hour of our death. Amen.

Wisdom without Words

Readings: Exod 32:7-14; John 5:31-47

Scripture:
They forgot the God who had saved them,
  who had done great deeds in Egypt. (Ps 106:21)

Reflection: "Pray" appears at the top of my to-do list every day, automatically added by my task management system. In part it is a reminder of where my life, and so my day, begins and ends: in God. I don't want to forget God, so as I do with other things I don't want to forget, I put God on my to-do list. I want to say that God is front and center, a high priority in my life. But I wonder if the to-do list prayers have become my golden calf. Have I made an image of God so small that I can send him to "done" for the day with a click?

Henri Nouwen wrote that spiritual formation is the painful and slow process of discovering God's incomprehensibility. God, he says, cannot be reduced to a single idea or concept, that all we can hope for is a sort of learned ignorance, a wisdom that we cannot put into words. In today's gospel Jesus challenges the Pharisees who think they can scour the Scriptures to find eternal life, limiting their search for God to the pages of a book.

Get your head out of the books and come to me, live this life, says Jesus. How else will you know in what to believe?

Do not consign him to the corners, to be ritually dispensed with on a to-do list, spiritual or otherwise, or hidden away when a book is closed. It's not that prayer shouldn't be on my list, nor that I should fail to hear God's word in the Scriptures, but I hear God asking me if I shouldn't be looking for him in everything on my list and off, from the grading of papers to the afternoon meetings to the student I run into in the grocery store: *"You should know more about me than you can put down in words."*

Meditation: Are there times when you find yourself checking God off the list of to-dos? How can you find ways to see God at work in the things on your calendar and in your everyday tasks?

Prayer: God, help us to lift our eyes from our books and lists and calendars. Grant us the eyes to see you in every encounter and every task in our day.

Meditating on Two Standards

Readings: Wis 2:1a, 12-22; John 7:1-2, 10, 25-30

Scripture:
". . . [L]et us put him to the test
that we may have proof of his gentleness
and try his patience." (Wis 2:19)

Reflection: In the middle of the second week of St. Ignatius of Loyola's *Spiritual Exercises* there is a meditation called "Two Standards." The exercitant is asked to meditate on two armies amassed on a plain far below, Christ's standard flying on one side, Lucifer's on the other. Ask for the grace, Ignatius advises, to be able to recognize the difference, to know where to plant your own standard.

It is tempting to imagine a battle scene like that in some epic movie, where the point of view is the high ground, colorful flags are snapping crisply as the two sides flow toward each other. It is easy to see who is who from this vantage point, easy to choose sides.

But as Ignatius the soldier well knew, a battle is much messier when one is on the ground. There is noise and dust and distraction. The banners are hard to spot at times, and enemies look not so different from friends. We must trust that the position set before the battle is the one we keep. So, too, in my life. There remain the two choices: life and death, good and evil, light and darkness, God and eternal emptiness. I have made my choice, planted my flag. But real life puts me to the test when I look for whom to follow.

The psalmist has advice for me. The Lord is close to the brokenhearted, those who are crushed in spirit, those who work for justice. So these are the banners I can look for on the ground. I can watch for the brokenhearted, for those who are troubled, those for whom justice is yet to be realized. There, in the midst of the lowly, I will find Christ.

Meditation: The first reading from the book of Wisdom says of the just one that his life is not like others. How is your life different because you follow Christ? How has whom you know in your day-to-day life changed over the course of this Lent?

Prayer: Grant us a share of your patience, God. Draw us close to you when we are broken in spirit and troubled, when we long for the justice and mercy that the world will not give.

Lion's Prey

Readings: Jer 11:18-20; John 7:40-53

Scripture:
O LORD, my God, in you I take refuge;
  save me from all my pursuers and rescue me,
Lest I become like the lion's prey. (Ps 7:2-3a)

Reflection: I woke to hear the horses stamping, shifting uneasily from foot to foot. My two sons and my husband were sleeping, rolled in blankets on the ground nearby, camping for the night with friends who live up the canyon from my dad's farm. We had talked on the ride out about all the wildlife that lived out of sight: the snakes and spiders, the coyotes and the mountain lions. What had seemed magical in daylight suddenly felt menacing during the dark of night.

The howling coyotes drew nearer, the horses grew more nervous, until I heard something rustling in the brush nearby. Without a thought, I pulled the boys nearer, putting my body between them and whatever might be out there. With their father and I curled around them, they slept secure the whole night through.

Every time I hear the seventh psalm, I think about that night, when the notion that I was lion's prey ceased to be metaphor and became all too real. When I grasped more deeply what it meant to be living in a darkness so profound

I cannot see what might be stalking me, to live without protection, far from help or shelter. And yet the psalmist promises that God will be as a shield before me.

Do not be tempted to treat the promises of this psalm as mere "froth and bubble," said St. John Chrysostom in a commentary. We may be pursued by the forces of evil, but those who burn with the Spirit's fire and hold lamps that can never be extinguished cannot be touched. So when evil draws close, I imagine God reaching for me in the darkness, pulling me close, and putting his body between me and whatever lions lie in wait, metaphorical or literal.

Meditation: When have you felt the need for God's protection? What menaces do you most fear?

Prayer: God, you are as a shield before us, as a haven of light in the darkness. Hold us close, that the evils that stalk this world may never touch us.

Stumbling into the Light

Readings: Ezek 37:12-14; Rom 8:8-11; John 11:1-45 or 11:3-7, 17, 20-27, 33b-45

Scripture:
He cried out in a loud voice, "Lazarus, come out!" (John 11:43)

Reflection: It's not (quite) Easter, yet having grown up with the knowledge of the resurrection I cannot help but hear in these readings a foreshadowing of the passion and the resurrection. Thomas is ready to go to Jerusalem and die with Jesus, the women are faith-filled in the face of death, and Lazarus lies in a tomb, to be restored to life. I know how the story ends, so at some level I'm untroubled by Martha and Mary's grief, unmoved by Thomas's determination to stick with Jesus come what may, unsurprised when Lazarus rises from the dead.

But the season has us linger in the doorway between death and life, to imagine again and again what it is like to have the Spirit breathing life into us, to rise. I recall John Updike's poem "Seven Stanzas at Easter." He warns against seeing the events of the paschal mystery as parables or pious legends, of prettying them up to make them more tolerable. Stand at the entrance to the tomb, he says, feel the weight of the rock and hear the grunting of those who struggle to unseal it. See a man tied hand and foot in linen emerge, stumbling into the light.

Lent or not, I live in this liminal space, believing in the resurrection, hoping that I, too, will be brought back to life in the end, pulled from the depths of sin. Again and again, Jesus calls me, and I stumble out of the tomb into the unbearable light. I might be unsurprised at my rescue, but let me never be anything less than stunned to be breathing again.

Meditation: The stories of the events leading to Jesus' passion, death, and resurrection are so familiar it can be hard to hear them afresh. Read through today's gospel. What catches your eye? What surprises you that you haven't thought about in several—many—years?

Prayer: We cry to you from the depths, O Lord, and beg you to untie the bonds of sin that confine us. Call us into the light, that we might once again proclaim your glory.

March 30: Monday of the Fifth Week of Lent

Waiting on Mercy

Readings: Dan 13:1-9, 15-17, 19-30, 33-62 or 13:41c-62; John 8:1-11

Scripture:
"Let the one among you who is without sin be the first to throw a stone at her." (John 8:7b)

Reflection: As a teacher I know the power of a well-timed question, and of waiting for its answer. Asking questions like that can be hard on students, whose grasp on the material is not yet secure; they hesitate to respond. Waiting quietly for an answer can be hard on the teachers, as we want to help, we want to be doing something. But sometimes the work of wringing out an answer to a question can teach a student more than I can do in an hour-long lecture. So I stand there awkwardly, and wait.

Jesus is willing to ask the questions, and to wait, to wait for the onlookers to search their hearts, to wait for them to cede their judgment to his. For all that I'm willing to ask questions and wait in my classroom, I'm sometimes less willing to ask and wait in the rest of my life. I tap the horn at the car in front of me, annoyed at its driver who has failed to see that the red light has flipped to green. The car finally budges and heads up the road at a crawl. Having no stones to cast, I reach for the horn again, jumping to judgment with-

72 *Monday of the Fifth Week of Lent*

out once recalling how it feels to be caught lost in thought while waiting for the light to turn or needing to crawl along looking for an address. I am not without sin.

In Graham Greene's novel *Brighton Rock*, there is a scene in the confessional where a young woman is wondering if her late husband is damned, or perhaps if she is. The priest listens patiently to her and finally wheezes back at her that neither he, nor she, nor any of us can grasp the appalling strangeness of God's mercy. All we can do is wait. Wait to judge. Wait for the mercy we hope will be ours.

Meditation: Where in your life are you tempted to jump to judgment and then throw stones at others? Can you ask Jesus to wait with you until you are ready to let judgment go in favor of mercy?

Prayer: God of mercy, keep our sins from clouding our sight. Grant us the patience to suspend our judgment of our brothers and sisters and the courage to forgive those who have wounded us.

Lift High the Cross

Readings: Num 21:4-9; John 8:21-30

Scripture:
Moses accordingly made a bronze serpent . . . and whenever anyone who had been bitten by a serpent looked at [it], he lived. (Num 21:9)

Reflection: When I hear "take up your cross," I tend to think of the sorts of crosses I wouldn't want to carry, the difficult things we are asked to bear either for ourselves or others. Crosses are burdens, they can wear out my patience like the Israelites. But in the first reading, we hear how Moses hoists the bronze serpent aloft, and the people who see it are healed of the serpent's bite. Jesus says we will raise him high and, seeing him for who he is, be healed of our sins. These crosses we are entrusted with are not solely burdens but signposts: healing can be found here.

Pope Francis has often referred to the church as a field hospital, a source of hope for the suffering and a place of healing, mercy, and forgiveness. This, he says, is the primary and fundamental mission of the church. He is clear that he sees this mission as being broader than the sacramental realities that the church provides; the church's vocation of mercy is more than the offering of the sacrament of reconciliation. We, the people of God, each and every one of us, are called to heal the sick, to tend to the dying, to provide for the desperate, to reconcile the divided. We are expected not just to carry a cross but to be a sign of the cross, to be Christ's hands and feet. Like a field hospital we are expected to be at the front, in the thick of the struggle. It is a place of risk, not of safety.

Taking a cue from the traditional Lenten hymn that begins, "Lift high the cross, the love of Christ proclaim . . . ," let us each day lift high the cross, to make the love of Christ not only visible but tangible.

Meditation: How do we lift high the cross as a sign that healing can be found here? Recall a moment when you made God's healing power visible and accessible to those in need. Where have you seen the cross and followed it to find healing in body, mind, or spirit?

Prayer: Lord, strengthen our arms, that we might lift high your cross. Make us a sign of hope to those in desperate need, a sign of unity to the divided, and a sign of peace to the nations.

Blessed Is the Lord

Readings: Dan 3:14-20, 91-92, 95; John 8:31-42

Scripture:
"Blessed are you in the firmament of heaven,
 praiseworthy and glorious forever." (Dan 3:56)

Reflection: I have pinned to the board in my office a few of those lovingly created construction paper cards from when my kids were in preschool. The cards are fragile after so many years, but I still delight in reading them to remind myself of the many ways I've been loved, from the acrostics that described me as "lively" and "curious" to the flower petals that counted the books we read together. On my toughest days as a parent, when I wondered if my children really loved me, I could read the litanies on my wall. *I love that you read to me, I love that you let me cook.*

In today's gospel I hear Jesus asking his followers that same question: Do you love me? How much? As much as Abraham? Enough to listen to my words? The three young men in the furnace have an answer to that question too. How much do they love God? So much that they tell Nebuchadnezzar that should God not spare them this fiery fate, they will not recant and worship something less. In the furnace the three young men cry out their love, seeing God manifest in the heavens, in the depths, on his throne, in his temple.

And I suspect that, like me, God delights in hearing how he is loved.

I am certain that God's love for me—for us—does not change. We are beloved children of God. I'm certain, too, that I love God. But can I count all the ways I am loved and love in return? Blessed are you, O Lord, who made the snowdrops that cascade down the hillside near my office. Blessed are you, O Lord, for the students who enliven my day. Blessed are you, O Lord, who feed me with your Body and Blood, praiseworthy and glorious forever.

Meditation: What would you praise the Lord for? Try writing or praying aloud a litany of the things you are grateful God has done for you in your own life. Do not lose sight of the small miracles—the green lights when you are running late for work—amid the awe-inspiring wonders of the firmament of heaven.

Prayer: Blessed are you, O Lord, in the firmament of heaven, for the guidepost of your Word. Blessed are you, O Lord, in your holy temple, for your Body and Blood that nourish us. Praiseworthy and glorious before all, forever.

April 2: Thursday of the Fifth Week of Lent

Unbound by Time

Readings: Gen 17:3-9; John 8:51-59

Scripture:
He remembers forever his covenant
which he made binding for a thousand generations.
   (Ps 105:8)

Reflection: The Liturgy of the Hours is dotted with the "Glory Be." This prayer opens every hour, is recited at the end of every psalm and canticle. The final words of this familiar doxology are on my lips dozens of times each day: "As it was in the beginning, is now and will be forever." I am reminded again and again that in times past and times present, even before time began, God is immutable, eternal, and mysteriously triune. Yet I am so wrapped up in secular time, tied to calendars and clocks, that like the onlookers in John's gospel, who are puzzled by Jesus' claim to know Abraham, I struggle with the idea of God who brushes aside time's limitations and is unbound by its linearity.

As a scientist, I know something of time and how it is measured. One second is defined as the time it takes for a particular atom (Cs-133) held at absolute zero to move between two states 9 billion, 192 million, 631 thousand, 770 times. As a mother, I know something of time and how it passes. There is no going back, only forward; I cannot stretch it out at will—the baby once asleep on my shoulder is now backing out of the driveway to head to Montana.

But here—in the Scriptures—and there—on the altar—we are offered the chance to become as God is, unbound by time. It's not about what we know, but who we know and who knows us. *Know me, know the Father and all limits are off*, says Jesus. *Life eternal is yours.* But even should I fail of this remembrance, be unable to grasp the mystery of God outside of time, God promises to never forget me, not for a second.

Meditation: The Scriptures, God's Word, let us move freely into time past and time future, to stand with Abraham at the moment God invokes his covenant, to see with St. John what awaits us in heaven. Pick a familiar story in the Scriptures and ask God to invite you to be present in that moment. Use all your senses. What do you hear, smell, taste, see, touch? How did you come to know God more deeply in that moment?

Prayer: Glory be to the Father, and to the Son, and to the Holy Spirit, as it was in the beginning, is now and will be forever.

Stones before the Lord

Readings: Jer 20:10-13; John 10:31-42

Scripture:
"I have shown you many good works from my Father. For which of these are you trying to stone me?" (John 10:32b)

"I tell you, if they keep silent, the stones will cry out!" (Luke 19:40b)

Reflection: Both the psalm and the gospel for the day speak of stones: of God as stone, of the stones the onlookers picked up, intending to stone Jesus. We tend to think of stones as quintessentially lifeless, as dead, unable to speak, but as Jesus reminds us in Luke's gospel (Luke 19:40), even the stones can cry out. It is tempting to hear Jesus' exclamation in Luke as hyperbole or metaphor—or as a miracle he might perform. But to geologists and planetary scientists, rocks do have voices. Meteorites, the stones that arrive from outside Earth's bounds, have much to say. They can tell us where they came from, Mars or the moon or some asteroid, and what they experienced in their journey here. Their stories cannot be silenced or erased, as they are part of their very being, written in their mineral composition and properties.

The psalm today presents the image of God, the living God, as rock. *My God, my rock of refuge. O Lord, my rock.* God, who is Truth, cannot be silenced. Like the rocks that crash onto the earth, what God is, where God comes from, all God has done for us is embedded in his very being. Even if the onlookers had stoned Jesus, the living Word is as rock, always crying aloud who and what he is.

But it's not just that Christ cannot be silenced. St. Peter tells us we are living stones built into Christ's Body (1 Pet 2:5). So, too, by our very nature we cannot be silenced. We are created to be ever proclaiming God's Word, the Good News that is Jesus, and praising him with full voice. Should our voices be silenced, we still are called to show forth the truth of God's glory by our deeds. Feed the hungry, accompany those in prison, shelter those in need. Look around you, are not the living stones crying out, "Here is the Lord"?

Meditation: Where do you hear the voice of God in the people around you? Who is preaching with words, who by deeds, who by their being? How are you a living stone? What are you saying, what are you doing, to declare the glory of God?

Prayer: God, you have built your church of living stones. Help us to proclaim your praises to the world and make your glory evident in everyone we meet.

April 4: Saturday of the Fifth Week of Lent

Walking Wounded

Readings: Ezek 37:21-28; John 11:45-56

Scripture:
Shouting, they shall mount the heights of Zion,
  they shall come streaming to the LORD's blessings.
  (Jer 31:12a)

Reflection: In these last few days of Lent, I am reminded of
Marie Howe's poem "The Star Market." She writes evoca-
tively of a local market, seeing figures from the Scriptures at
every turn: here the man whose friends might have lowered
him by ropes to get him before Jesus, there the woman so
desperate to be healed she dared reach out to touch Jesus'
cloak. The narrator seems uneasy at finding herself among
these people Jesus loved, who stumble through the market
in search of what they need for their daily lives.

Whether we were stumbling about in the dark or streaming in from our everyday lives, we came to Lent in search of
what we needed to sustain us and our relationship with God.
We dared to reach out to touch grace, hoping for the blessings promised us in Jeremiah's canticle—the grain, the wine,
and the oil. We came to eat of Christ's Body and drink of his
Blood, to be nourished at the eucharistic table. We came for
the healing salve of the sacrament of reconciliation.

Tomorrow we enter Holy Week, where the work of this Lent winds to an end. This day will undoubtedly begin as most of my Saturdays begin. I will clear the table of accumulated mail and throw the sheets and towels in the wash, tidying up the detritus of a week gone by. On this Saturday in particular, I will make time to take a walk with God, to gather up what Lent has sown in me over these past five weeks. I will pray for the grace—and the courage—to see where I have been fed, where my thirst for God has been slaked, where I have been consoled and healed. I will pray for the grace to give over stumbling and enter into these holy days singing of God's tremendous deeds.

Meditation: As you enter into Holy Week, what have been the blessings of this Lent for you? Where have you been fed, given feet to dance, been consoled and had your soul salved? Where are you no longer walking as one wounded but as one who has been seen and touched by God?

Prayer: Grant us the blessings you promised Jeremiah, O Lord. May we always be fed at your table and find solace in your healing Word. May the work you have done in us this Lent make us radiant with joy and ready to praise your glory.

Eclipsed

Readings: Matt 21:1-11; Isa 50:4-7; Phil 2:6-11; Matt 26:14–27:66 or 27:11-54

Scripture:
The earth quaked, rocks were split, tombs were opened. (Matt 27:51b)

Reflection: "Aunt Chel," my niece said, "something is wrong with the sun." In the dry California canyon where she lives, I was worried about fire. So I took her hand and we went outside to check for smoke. She was right, the light wasn't quite right for midday, yet there was no sign of a fire. The skies were clear, the sun in its usual spot, but it was definitely growing darker. And the shadows looked funny. I felt uneasy, off kilter, and uncertain of what was happening. I looked more closely at the shadow the almond tree cast on the walkway, and suddenly I understood. "We are having an eclipse," I told her, reassuring her that nothing was wrong, that the sun would return in full force in a few hours.

I know how the passion comes out. Jesus goes to his death, as inexorably as the moon crossed between the earth and the sun that afternoon, whether we knew ahead of time it was happening or not. He dies, he is buried. He rises. The sun shines brilliantly. I can listen to the passion without worrying about how it will all end.

In our almost two thousand years of celebrating these holy days of our salvation, I wonder if we've lost any sense of that unsettled feeling the disciples must have had. Seeing signs that suggested things were not as they had been, or should be, but not knowing quite what they meant and how it would all come out. Can I listen to the passion, present to its reality, without mentally racing on ahead to the ending? Worried I have let my sure knowledge of the resurrection eclipse the mystery, I tune my ears to the voices of those unsure and those shaken by what is taking place: Pilate and his wife, Peter, the centurions at the cross. For I cannot welcome the Light, if I have not first plunged into the darkness.

Meditation: Pray for the grace to walk the passion slowly and reverently, to look beyond the high points and seek out the moments when faith falters, when underlying assumptions are shaken. Listen, too, for the times when tiny sparks of uncertainty burst into flames of recognition—"Clearly, this is the Son of God!"

Prayer: Lord God, give us the courage to hear your passion as though for the first time. Grant that we might for this moment stand in the darkness that enveloped the world before you redeemed it, that we might more deeply experience the dawning of our new life in the days to come.

The Smell of the Shepherd

Readings: Isa 42:1-7; John 12:1-11

Scripture:
Mary took a liter of costly perfumed oil made from genuine aromatic nard and anointed the feet of Jesus and dried them with her hair; the house was filled with the fragrance of the oil. (John 12:3)

Reflection: The ointment's fragrance filled the air wherever I walked that night. My hands had been drenched in the chrism my pastor applied with such abundance at the Easter Vigil that the chrismarium he handed back to me after anointing each candidate for baptism had been covered in the sacred oil. Even a thorough hand washing in the sacristy had not banished the scent.

Pope Francis has often said those called to proclaim the Gospel should "smell of the sheep"—but I wonder if we also all ought not to smell of the shepherd. For we, too, were anointed at our baptism to be as Christ: priest, prophet, and king. How do we carry that fragrance out into the world? In his apostolic exhortation *Evangelii Gaudium*, Pope Francis suggests that beauty plays a role, both the beauty of the liturgy and the beauty of lives that take seriously the call to spread goodness and joy, willing to celebrate the smallest things. We are called to give of this joy extravagantly, even to the point of impractically. We are encouraged not to worry whether the gifts we give yield the perfect fruit. We simply offer what we can and are delighted in the new life that grows, even if it is incomplete or imperfect.

Mary of Bethany knelt at Jesus' feet, anointing him with her extravagant gift of beautiful-smelling oil. I can't imagine the fragrance didn't linger on her hands too. Nor can I imagine that she didn't carry the smell of the Shepherd with her everywhere she went for the rest of her life, redolent of the joy of the Gospel.

Meditation: What aspect of your baptismal anointing do you feel most strongly called toward: priest, prophet, or king? Which aspects are you perhaps neglecting or unwilling to exercise?

Prayer: May we embrace our baptismal anointing as priest, prophet, and king. May our lives be redolent of joy in the Gospel, and may we ever carry with us the fragrance of Christ.

April 7: Tuesday of Holy Week

To Be All Flame

Readings: Isa 49:1-6; John 13:21-33, 36-38

Scripture:
I will make you a light to the nations,
    that my salvation may reach to the ends of the earth.
        (Isa 49:6b)

Reflection: One of my favorite stories from the fifteen-hundred-year-old collection of wisdom from the Desert Fathers and Mothers is of Abba Lot and Abba Joseph of Panephysis. One day Abba Lot came to Abba Joseph for advice. "I fast, I pray, I live in peace," he said. "What else should I do?" Abba Joseph lifted his hands to heaven. Flames danced at his fingertips, and he turned to Abba Lot and said, "If you wish, you can become all flame."

We have fasted and prayed and given alms this Lent. What more is expected of us? We hear in Isaiah that we are to be a light to the nations, a light visible to the ends of the earth. We can be all flame, if we wish, says Abba Joseph. But how? Writing on the psalms, St. Augustine points out that our light does not come from ourselves; it is the Lord who sets our lamps alight. Lift up your hands to heaven and pray to be alight, to be all flame.

To pray to be light is risky. We are not asking for a light to see by, for something to hold up that we might illuminate our failings or find the safe path—as perilous as those prayers might be. We are asking to *be* light that others can see by, to be set on fire by the Lord, and what is set aflame is utterly transformed. Christ dares me to lay aside my own desires and let him light my lamp, remaking me in ways I cannot imagine. If I wish, I could become all flame. But do I wish?

Meditation: Where are the cracks in your stony heart through which the light is eager to pour forth? What would you imagine it would be like to be "all flame" for the Gospel? What would change in your life? What would change in your inmost being?

Prayer: We have fasted and prayed and given generously to those in need, O Lord. Now we ask to be set aflame, that we might be transformed, that we might become light from Light.

A Terrible Grace

Readings: Isa 50:4-9a; Matt 26:14-25

Scripture:
"Surely it is not I, Lord?" (Matt 26:22b)

Reflection: As I dash through this hectic week, juggling a job that takes no notice of the liturgical season with preparing for liturgies that cry out for everything I have and more, I can sometimes find it hard to stifle my to-do list long enough to spend prayerful time with these last Lenten readings. I struggle to do as the disciples did and recline at the table with Jesus, unhurried, allowing myself one last dollop of Lenten grace.

Besides, emerging from Lent's disciplines, standing at the edge of the Triduum, I'm frankly tempted to a bit of Isaiah's satisfaction: I have not rebelled, I have not turned back. My well-trained tongue knows what to say to my God. But praying with the gospel story of Judas's betrayal makes me face uncomfortable truths. *Surely it is not I, Lord?*

I need to be able to hear these readings, not only as one who has sinned and been forgiven but as one who will sin again. Not as one who once betrayed Jesus but as one who will betray him again. Not as one who has repented but as one who will need to repent of sins and betrayals, large and small, again and again. To listen as one who has been re-deemed. Lent may have ended, but my journey as a re-deemed sinner has not. *Surely it is not I, Lord.* Not today, perhaps, nor even tomorrow, but the time will surely come when I will rebel, will once again turn my back on God.

For all of this, I hear in these readings that God will not reject me, not spurn those he claims for his own. There is no turning back from that terrible grace. Thank God.

Meditation: We walk out of Lent as we walked into it, re-deemed sinners, beloved of God. Where are you tempted to complacency—or its opposite? Where are you too hard on yourself? Where do you desire God to hold you up in the days that will follow, into Easter and beyond? What has God accomplished in your life this Lent, and what does he wish to make manifest to you in the crucible of the Triduum?

Prayer: God, help us to set aside the demands of our lives and recline at the table of your Word and your Body through these holy days. May our hearts not be complacent, and may our ears be open to hear uncomfortable truths.

Not Metaphor, but Reality

Readings: Exod 12:1-8, 11-14; 1 Cor 11:23-26; John 13:1-15

Scripture:
As I have done for you, you should also do. (John 13:15b)

Reflection: The birth of my second son was fast and tumultuous. When it was all over, his heart once again beating strongly and all the necessary medical tasks for us both tended to, the obstetrician who had delivered him filled a basin with warm water and brought me a fresh towel with which to wash my face. It was unexpected, and like Peter when Jesus knelt at his feet, I was taken aback. *I'm fine. I don't need this done*, I thought. Except I did.

I'm always tempted on Holy Thursday to let my attention be seized by St. Paul's mandate to the Corinthians to break the bread and drink the cup that is Christ's Body and Blood in remembrance of his death and resurrection, to focus on the incredible gift of the Eucharist that we enact daily on altars around the world. This once-a-year washing of the feet, towels piled on the altar and the choir singing meditatively, can feel like something extra, an embellishment for the Triduum. It's nice, but not needed. Except it is.

For here is the one moment in the liturgical year when the two dimensions of the Eucharist come crashing together. The Eucharist is not just the summit of our lives as Christians; it is the font as well. Here, with literal water poured out on the steps of the altar where we will shortly literally encounter Christ, we show each other what we are about, what it means to be Christ. The aching feet I have been standing on to teach, then to rehearse, and now to celebrate will be soothed in the warm water. What I will eat and drink will in truth feed a body that has missed lunch and dinner as much as it will feed my soul. These are not metaphors we are playing out here, but hard realities, the water as much as the bread and the wine. We wash each other, feed each other. We do these things, and so we remember. We remember, and so we do.

Meditation: How often do you find yourself responding to an offer of assistance with a quick, "Thanks, but I don't need any help"? We are often happy to help but reluctant to accept care in return. What stops you from accepting God's tender care and help?

Prayer: You have commanded us to care for one another's daily needs. Grant us the strength to bend down before our sisters and brothers and wash their feet, and the humility to let our feet be washed in return.

In Manus Tuas

Readings: Isa 52:13–53:12; Heb 4:14-16; 5:7-9; John 18:1–19:42

Scripture:
Into your hands I commend my spirit;
  you will redeem me, O LORD, O faithful God. (Ps 31:6)

Reflection: The college where I work houses a large collection of late medieval devotional prayer books, which one of the courses I teach occasionally uses. My favorite is the fifteenth-century *Marquand Book of Hours,* not because of the inarguable beauty of its illustrations but because of a single smudged page. The ink and coloring on the lower left-hand side of the first page of Compline—Night Prayer—has been worn away and the corner is smudged with use. It is just this page that shows such wear, rubbed raw by the thumbs of its owner who opened it each night to pray before bed: *In manus tuas commendabo spiritum meum.* Into your hands I commend my spirit.

Last night, beginning in a dark church stripped to the bone, the incense from the Mass of the Last Supper still lurking in the corners, my community prayed in these age-old words to commend ourselves to God. *Into your hands I commend my spirit.* I am consoled to hear these words prayed by my community, heartened by the whispers of them I hear lingering between the covers of those fifteenth-century devotionals, and encouraged when I encounter them in the psalms we will sing at today's liturgies. What I cannot always pray for myself, I can pray for others and know that others will do the same for me, across time and space.

I marvel that these words from Psalm 31 were on Jesus' lips on the cross, were clung to each night by an unknown man or woman in fifteenth-century Rome, and are the same words we still pray in the modern church's Night Prayer. All of us praying them at the edge of darkness, letting go of our own vigil, trusting that God will keep vigil in our stead, our lives in the hands of our ever-faithful God, whether we have placed them there or not.

Meditation: What might stop you from handing your life over to God? For just the night, or for the full course of your days. If you don't already pray the Liturgy of the Hours, consider praying just Night Prayer before you go to sleep tonight.

Prayer: Into your hands, O Lord, we commend our lives, our spirits, and our souls. Keep watch for us when the darkness encroaches, and keep us safe under your wings when we can no longer keep vigil for ourselves.

Ordinary Glory

Readings: Gen 1:1–2:2 or 1:1, 26-31a; Gen 22:1-18 or 22:1-2, 9a, 10-13, 15-18; Exod 14:15–15:1; Isa 54:5-14; 55:1-11; Bar 3:9-15, 32–4:4; Ezek 36:16-17a, 18-28; Rom 6:3-11; Matt 28:1-10

Scripture:
Seek the LORD while he may be found,
call him while he is near. (Isa 55:6)

The living, the living give you thanks, / as I do today.
The LORD is there to save us. / We shall play our music
In the house of the LORD / all the days of our life.
  (Isa 38:19a, 20)

Reflection: Holy Saturday morning finds us suspended between yesterday's achingly difficult liturgy of the Lord's passion and the triumphant singing of the *Exsultet* tonight. It can be a welcome taste of ordinary time in the midst of these emotionally charged days. I'll freely admit to a sense of relief that for a few hours I'm facing the week's laundry and the breakfast dishes, and not Christ on the cross, or even the risen Christ in glory.

Theologian Karl Rahner, SJ, suggested that Holy Saturday makes sacred and obvious where we live all the time, suspended between the death that has been vanquished and the eternal life in glory we are promised. The trick of it, he says, is not to regard the ordinariness with resignation, as a routine to be gotten through. We are not confined or beaten down by our mundane existence, but buoyed in it on the hope of eternal life.

To practice balancing on this subtle edge is a challenge. I am, as I am every year, exhausted by Lent's rigor, wrung out by the liturgies of Holy Week. I hear in the canticle from Isaiah offered today at Morning Prayer that same tension between resigned exhaustion—*I moan like a dove, my eyes grow weak*—and expectant hope—*the living, the living give you thanks* (Isa 38:14, 19).

So today is a day to listen to the rhythm of our ordinary life with ears attuned to tonight's resounding alleluias, with memories of the celebration of the Passion yet fresh. To sing "O Sacred Head Surrounded" one moment and hum an Easter alleluia with the next breath. To hold gratefully to life, even in the face of exhaustion and weakness. To know how to let ourselves be emptied out, that we might, with our last breath, be filled with grace and the Holy Spirit.

Meditation: Where are the routines in your life that try your patience? Where might you ask God to strengthen your hope, to be your surety when you are overwhelmed?

Prayer: Brighten our ordinary days, O Lord, with your light. Breathe in us, that we might find hope when we are stretched to our limit, and give us strength, that we might sing to you all the days of our life.

The Earth Has Been Shaken

Readings: Acts 10:34a, 37-43; Col 3:1-4 or 1 Cor 5:6b-8; John 20:1-9 or Matt 28:1-10

Scripture:
And behold, there was a great earthquake; for an angel of the Lord descended from heaven, approached, rolled back the stone, and sat upon it. (Matt 28:2)

Reflection: I know it is Easter from the moment I set foot in the church, all light and sparkling bright. White lilies crowd the altar, the crowd buzzes with joy. The plain wood processional cross is nearly overshadowed by the altar servers and deacon and priest all vested in white and gold. The lector holds the Good News aloft, gold ribbons gently fluttering as she walks. There are words of warm welcome.

But, behold, says the gospel, there has been a great earthquake. Why do I not see everything overset? Why are the pews not scattered like matchsticks, the altar covered in dust from a dome broken open to the sky, a great wind whipping the trees about? And instead of children dressed in their best for Easter brunch, why are there not people milling about in confusion and fear, their clothes torn and shoes unmatched in their haste to come see what happened here last night? There is an angel sitting on the steps of the altar reassuring us: do not be afraid. Inviting us: come and see. Pushing us back out: go and tell what you have seen.

In "An Expedition to the Pole," Annie Dillard wonders why we are so blithe about our faith. It is madness, she says, to come dressed in our finery; crash helmets are what we should don before praying to the all-powerful, ever-living God. Am I willing to meditate on the power revealed on that first Easter when God pierced the earth and ripped aside the curtain between life and death? Can I let the shock waves of that earth-shattering event knock me to the floor, as it did the centurions? I fear I will find the shimmering vestments, the rippling trumpets, and the lilies to be enough Easter, and shut out the sight of a world overturned by the shock of the resurrection, still shaking in fear and awe and joy.

So I pray to be greeted this year by an angel on the steps of the church, telling me not to fear the shaking ground, inviting me to come in and see the Lord. In the end, pushing me back out the door, so like the two Marys I might encounter Jesus, risen from the dead. I pray to see past Easter's glitter; rather, I beg, let me become all flame.

Meditation: Pray Psalm 97 with its images of an earth trembling, the mountains melting, and the earth rejoicing that the Lord is king. What do you desire to see this Easter?

Prayer: I believe in one Lord Jesus Christ,
the Only Begotten Son of God,
born of the Father before all ages.
God from God, Light from Light . . .

References

Introduction
Alden T. Solovy, "Sowing Light," in *This Grateful Heart: Psalms and Prayers for a New Day* (New York: CCAR Press, 2017).

February 26: Ash Wednesday
Ignatius of Loyola, Letter to Ascanio Colonna (Rome, April 25, 1543), http://gc36.org/saints-formed-grace-god/.

February 28: Friday after Ash Wednesday
Leonard Cohen, "Anthem," from *The Essential Leonard Cohen* (Legacy, 2002).

March 1: First Sunday of Lent
Vida D. Scudder, *Saint Catherine of Siena as Seen in Her Letters* (New York: J. M. Dent & Company, 1905), 305.

March 2: Monday of the First Week of Lent
C. S. Lewis, "The Weight of Glory," in *The Weight of Glory* (New York: Harper Collins, 2001), 47.

March 8: Second Sunday of Lent
Julian of Norwich, *Julian of Norwich: Showings*, trans. Edmund Colledge and James Walsh (New York: Paulist Press, 1977), 183.

March 9: Monday of the Second Week of Lent
Benedicta Ward, *The Sayings of the Desert Fathers: The Alphabetical Collection* (Kalamazoo, MI: Cistercian, 2004), 40.

March 11: Wednesday of the Second Week of Lent
Bernard Bangley, *Butler's Lives of the Saints: Concise, Modernized Edition* (Brewster, MA: Paraclete Press, 2005), 16.

March 13: Friday of the Second Week of Lent
Karl Rahner, SJ, "God of My Daily Routine," in *Encounters in Silence* (South Bend, IN: St. Augustine's Press, 1999).

March 15: Third Sunday of Lent
Augustine of Hippo, *Tractates on the Gospel of John*, 15.31, http://www.newadvent.org/fathers/1701015.htm.

March 16: Monday of the Third Week of Lent
Malcolm Muggeridge, *Christ and the Media* (Vancouver: Regent College Publishing, 2003).

March 17: Tuesday of the Third Week of Lent
Denise Levertov, "To Live in the Mercy of God," in *The Stream & the Sapphire: Selected Poems on Religious Themes* (New York: New Directions, 1997).

March 18: Wednesday of the Third Week of Lent
Augustine of Hippo, Sermon on 1 John 4:4-12, http://www.newadvent.org/fathers/170207.htm.
T. S. Eliot, "The Dry Salvages," in *Collected Poems 1909–1962* (London: Faber & Faber, 1990).

March 22: Fourth Sunday of Lent
Dietrich Bonhoeffer, "Costly Grace," in *The Cost of Discipleship* (New York: Touchstone, 1995).

March 25: The Annunciation of the Lord
Johann Baptist Metz, *Poverty of Spirit* (New York: Paulist Press, 1998).

March 27: Friday of the Fourth Week of Lent
Louis J. Puhl, SJ, *The Spiritual Exercises of St. Ignatius of Loyola* (Chicago: Loyola University Press, 1986).

March 28: Saturday of the Fourth Week of Lent
John Chrysostom, *Commentary on the Psalms, Vol. 1*, ed. Robert C. Hill (Brookline, MA: Holy Cross Orthodox Press, 2007), 117.

March 29: Fifth Sunday of Lent
John Updike, "Seven Stanzas at Easter," in *Collected Poems 1953–1993* (New York: Knopf, 1993), 20–21.

March 30: Monday of the Fifth Week of Lent
Graham Greene, *Brighton Rock* (London: Penguin Classics, 1991), 245–46.

April 4: Saturday of the Fifth Week of Lent
Marie Howe, "The Star Market," in *The Kingdom of Ordinary Time* (New York: Norton, 2008), 15.

April 6: Monday of Holy Week
Pope Francis, *Evangelii Gaudium*, The Joy of the Gospel (Vatican City: Libreria Editrice Vaticana, 2013), 24.

April 7: Tuesday of Holy Week
Benedicta Ward, *The Sayings of the Desert Fathers: The Alphabetical Collection* (Kalamazoo, MI: Cistercian, 2004), 103.

Augustine of Hippo, in *Psalms 1–50: Ancient Christian Commentary*, ed. Craig A. Blaising and Carmen S. Hardin (Downers Grove, IL: Intervarsity Press Academic, 2008), 140.

April 10: Friday of the Passion of the Lord (Good Friday)
Intimate Devotion, http://www.brynmawr.edu/library/exhibits/hours/.
Liturgy of the Hours, eBreviary, https://www.ebreviary.com/.

April 11: Holy Saturday and Easter Vigil
Karl Rahner, SJ, *The Great Church: The Best of Karl Rahner's Homilies, Sermons, and Meditations* (New York: Crossroad, 1994), 168–69.

April 12: Easter Sunday: The Resurrection of the Lord
Annie Dillard, "An Expedition to the Pole," in *Teaching a Stone to Talk: Expeditions and Encounters* (New York: Harper, 2013).